About This Book

Title: *Earth Changes*

Step: 6

Word Count: 251

Skills in Focus: Diphthongs /ow/ and /oi/

Tricky Words: natural, through, moves, volcano, erosion, magma

Ideas for Using This Book

Before Reading:

- **Comprehension:** Look at the title and cover image together. Walk through the pictures in the book with readers and have them make predictions about what they might learn while reading.
- **Accuracy:** Practice saying the tricky words listed on page 1.
- **Phonics:** Tell students they will read words with /ow/ and /oi/ diphthongs. Explain that a diphthong is two vowel sounds merged together. The letter combinations *oy* and *oi* make the same diphthong sound. The letters *ow* and *ou* make another sound. Write these letter combinations on a piece of paper. Then write the story words *ground*, *down*, *destroys*, and *soil*. Have readers point to the letter combinations making the diphthongs in each word. Then have readers look through the first few pages of the book to see if they can find any other words with /ow/ and /oi/ diphthongs.

During Reading:

- Have readers point under each word as they read it.
- **Decoding:** If readers are stuck on a word, help them say each sound and blend the sounds together smoothly. Point out words with /ow/ and /oi/ diphthongs as they appear. On pages 6 and 17, readers may need support with the phrases "down slowly" and "howls and blows." The letter combination *ow* makes a different sound in each word.
- **Comprehension:** Invite students to talk about what new things they are learning about Earth changes while reading. What are they learning that they didn't know before?

After Reading:

Discuss the book. Some ideas for questions:

- Where might you see Earth changing?
- What do you still wonder about Earth changes?

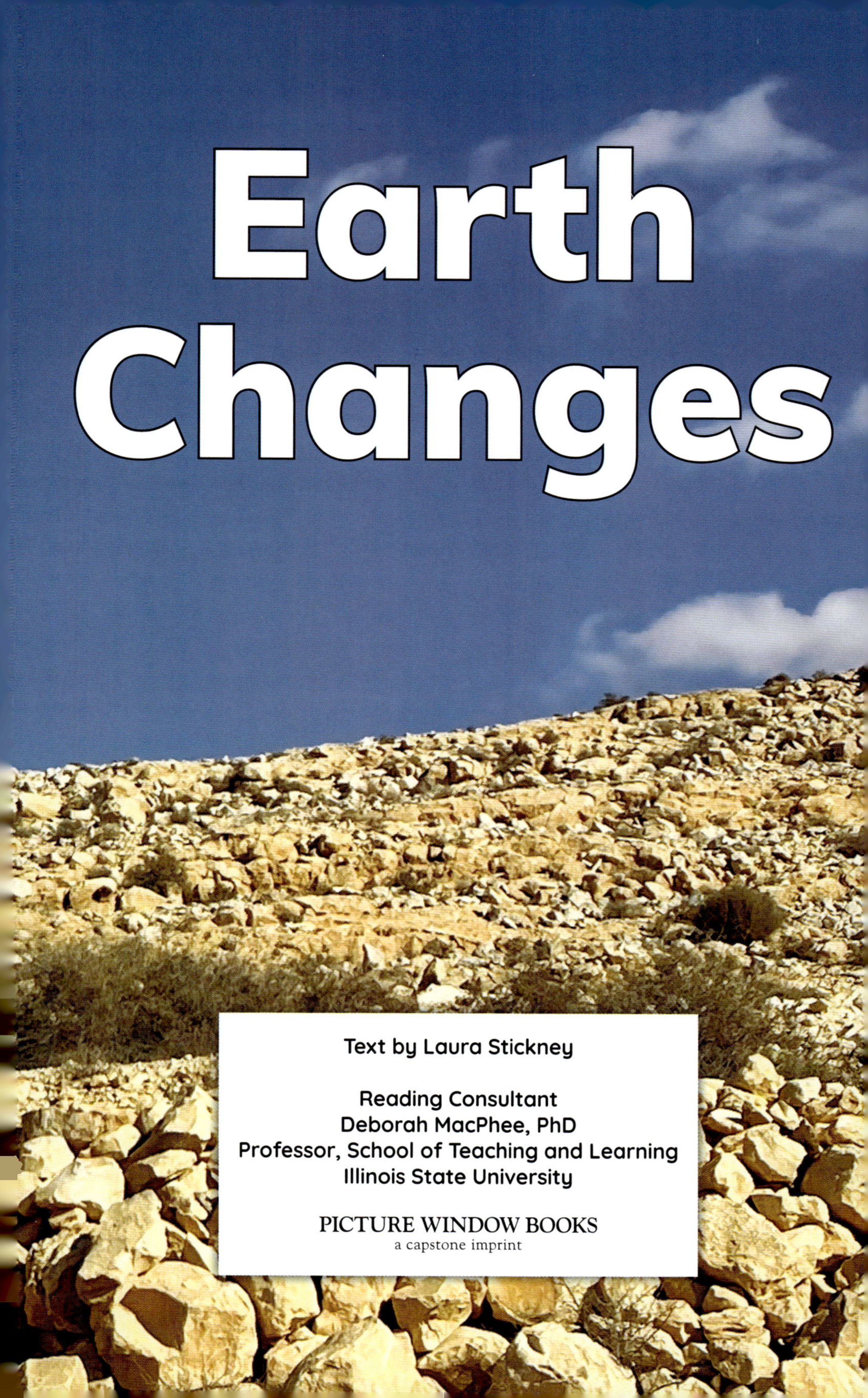

Earth Changes

Text by Laura Stickney

Reading Consultant
Deborah MacPhee, PhD
Professor, School of Teaching and Learning
Illinois State University

PICTURE WINDOW BOOKS
a capstone imprint

The ground under our feet changes all the time.

Natural forces make Earth's soil wear down.

Erosion

The ground wears down slowly over time. This is called erosion.

Water makes the soil moist. It pushes through the ground and breaks rocks apart.

Rain falls from clouds and wears down rocks over time.

Rocks and soil are found on the muddy ground near a river's mouth.

At some point on the river's path, the river picks up the rocks and soil.

It moves them around to new places.

Over time, water can carve out canyons in the ground.

Many years ago, water carved out the Grand Canyon.

Now, crowds enjoy the views there.

Wind wears down the ground too.

When the wind howls and blows, it shifts dirt around. It forms dusty brown dunes.

Wind and rain can change mountains.

They wear down rocks
around the mountain's sides.

This makes the rocks tumble and bounce down the mountain's slopes.

Volcanoes

A volcano is a mountain with a vent in Earth's surface.

Hot melted rock, or magma, lies deep underground inside a volcano.

When a volcano erupts, it sprays out magma and clouds of ash.

The magma turns into lava that boils and bubbles.

Lava burns the ground and destroys things in its path. Then it hardens into rock.

Asteroids

Some Earth changes are caused by asteroids. These are space rocks.

If an asteroid hits Earth, it makes a crater in the ground.

Look around. What do you notice about how Earth changes?

More Ideas:

Phonics Activity

Writing with /ow/ and /oi/ Diphthongs:

Ask readers to write a story using as many words as possible that have /ow/ and /oi/ diphthongs. The story can be as silly or as serious as readers want!

Suggested words:
/ow/ and /ou/: ground, our, around, clouds, down, howls, crowds, how, now
/oi/ and /oy/: soil, moist, asteroid, point, boils, enjoy

Extended Learning Activity

Observing Earth:

Have readers go outside and observe the ground or landscape around them. Ask them to think about what the ground looks like and how the land might have changed over time. Then have readers write or dictate a few sentences about their observations. Challenge readers to use words with /ow/ and /oi/ diphthongs in their sentences.

Published by Picture Window Books, an imprint of Capstone
1710 Roe Crest Drive, North Mankato, Minnesota 56003
capstonepub.com

Library of Congress Cataloging-in-Publication Data is available on the Library of Congress website.

ISBN: 9798875277863 (hardback)
ISBN: 9798875277825 (paperback)
ISBN: 9798875277801 (eBook PDF)

Image Credits: Getty: Andres Barrionuevo Lopez, 11, AnnaStills, 4–5, FamVeld, 8–9, back cover, Gani Pradana Ongko Prastowo, 1, 22–23, nazar_ab, 30–31, neil bowman, 10, nickehallgren, 15, Sergey Granev, 7, vovashevchuk, 17; Shutterstock: Abdulelah77, 16, Filip Fuxa, 12–13, Florian Nimsdorf, front cover, Fotema, 6, Framalicious, 28–29, ImageBank4u, 24–25, Ja Crispy, 18–19, Nicholas J Klein, 14, 32, Opus Mutus, 26–27, SERGUNello, 20–21, Studioktb, 2–3

Printed and bound in China. PO 6460